The Eskimos had
fifty-two names for
snow because it was
important to them:
there ought to be as
many for love.

Margaret Atwood's
little book of
selected quotes

You may not be able to alter reality, but you can alter your attitude towards it, and this, paradoxically, alters reality. Try it and see.

Margaret Atwood's little book of selected quotes

There is no fool like
an educated fool.

Margaret Atwood's
little book of
selected quotes

There is more than one kind of freedom," said Aunt Lydia. "Freedom to and freedom from. In the days of anarchy, it was freedom to. Now you are being given freedom from. Don't underrate it.

Margaret Atwood's little book of selected quotes

Maybe I don't really want to know what's going on. Maybe I'd rather not know. Maybe I couldn't bear to know. The Fall was a fall from innocence to knowledge.

Margaret Atwood's little book of selected quotes

Where do the
words go when we
have said them?

Margaret Atwood's
little book of
selected quotes

I want, I don't want.
How can one live with
such a heart?

Margaret Atwood's
little book of
selected quotes

Ignoring isn't the
same as ignorance,
you have to work at it.

Margaret Atwood's
little book of
selected quotes

Time has not stood still. It has washed over me, washed me away, as if I'm nothing more than a woman of sand, left by a careless child too near the water.

Margaret Atwood's little book of selected quotes

In the spring, at the end of the day, you should smell like dirt.

Margaret Atwood's little book of selected quotes

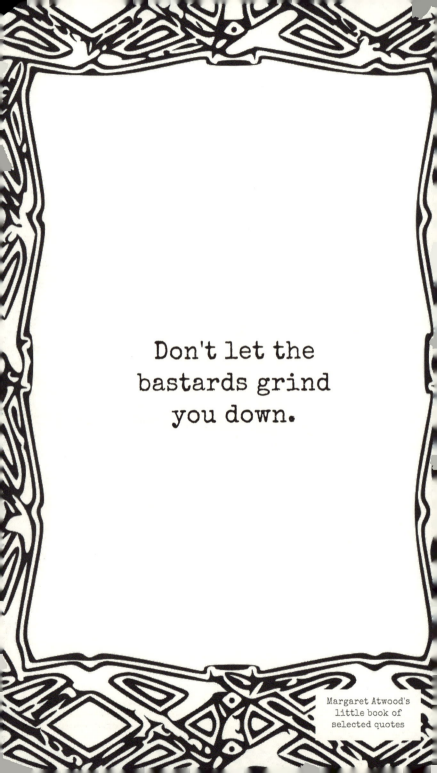

Don't let the
bastards grind
you down.

Margaret Atwood's
little book of
selected quotes

Don't sit down in the middle of the woods. If you're lost in the plot or blocked, retrace your steps to where you went wrong. Then take the other road. And/or change the person. Change the tense. Change the opening page.

Margaret Atwood's little book of selected quotes

Better never means
better for everyone...
It always means
worse, for some.

Margaret Atwood's
little book of
selected quotes

Little girls are
cute and small only
to adults. To one
another they are
not cute. They are
life-sized.

Margaret Atwood's
little book of
selected quotes

Without the light,
no chance; without
the dark, no dance.

Margaret Atwood's
little book of
selected quotes

This above all, to refuse to be a victim.

Margaret Atwood's
little book of
selected quotes

In the end, we'll all become stories.

Margaret Atwood's little book of selected quotes

I've never understood why people consider youth a time of freedom and joy. It's probably because they have forgotten their own.

Margaret Atwood's little book of selected quotes

I think calling it
climate change is
rather limiting.
I would rather call it
the everything change.

Margaret Atwood's
little book of
selected quotes

If he wants to be an asshole, it's a free country. Millions before him have made the same life choice.

Margaret Atwood's little book of selected quotes

If I love you, is that
a fact or a weapon?

Margaret Atwood's
little book of
selected quotes

While he writes, I feel
as if he is drawing me;
or not drawing me,
drawing on me – drawing
on my skin – not with the
pencil he is using, but
with an old-fashioned
goose pen, and not with
the quill end but with
the feather end. As if
hundreds of butterflies
have settled all over my
face, and are softly
opening and closing
their wings.

Margaret Atwood's
little book of
selected quotes

You can wipe your feet on me, twist my motives around all you like, you can dump millstones on my head and drown me in the river, but you can't get me out of the story. I'm the plot, babe, and don't ever forget it.

Margaret Atwood's little book of selected quotes

Men are afraid that women will laugh at them. Women are afraid that men will kill them.

Margaret Atwood's little book of selected quotes

The only way you can
write the truth is to
assume that what you set
down will never be read.
Not by any other person,
and not even by yourself
at some later date.
Otherwise you begin
excusing yourself. You
must see the writing as
emerging like a long
scroll of ink from the
index finger of your
right hand; you must see
your left hand erasing it.

Margaret Atwood's
little book of
selected quotes

Sooner or later, I hate to break it to you, you're gonna die, so how do you fill in the space between here and there? It's yours. Seize your space.

Margaret Atwood's little book of selected quotes

When we're young,
we like happy endings.
When we're a little
older, we think
happy endings are
unrealistic and so
we prefer bad but
credible endings. When
we're older still, we
realize happy endings
aren't so bad after all.

Margaret Atwood's
little book of
selected quotes

The astrologers would tell that the U.S. is ruled by fire and Canada is ruled by water. Short version: You pep us up, we cool you down.

Margaret Atwood's little book of selected quotes

At the very least
we want a witness.
We can't stand the
idea of our own
voices falling
silent finally,
like a radio
running down.

Margaret Atwood's
little book of
selected quotes

There were a lot of
gods. Gods always
come in handy,
they justify
almost anything.

Margaret Atwood's
little book of
selected quotes

We were the people who
were not in the papers.
We lived in the blank
white spaces at the
edges of print. It gave
us more freedom.
We lived in the gaps
between the stories.

Margaret Atwood's
little book of
selected quotes

I wanted to forget the
past, but it refused
to forget me;
it waited for sleep,
then cornered me.

Margaret Atwood's
little book of
selected quotes

But who can remember pain, once it's over? All that remains of it is a shadow, not in the mind even, in the flesh. Pain marks you, but too deep to see. Out of sight, out of mind.

Margaret Atwood's little book of selected quotes

If you get hungry
enough, they say,
you start eating
your own heart.

Margaret Atwood's
little book of
selected quotes

So much better to
travel than to
arrive.

Margaret Atwood's
little book of
selected quotes

The trickle-down theory of economics has it that it's good for rich people to get even richer because some of their wealth will trickle down, through their no doubt lavish spending, upon those who stand below them on the economic ladder. Notice that the metaphor is not that of a gushing waterfall but of a leaking tap: even the most optimistic endorsers of this concept do not picture very much real flow, as their language reveals.

Margaret Atwood's little book of selected quotes

Which of us can resist
the temptation of
being thought
indispensable?

Margaret Atwood's
little book of
selected quotes

Touch comes before sight, before speech. It is the first language and the last, and it always tells the truth.

Margaret Atwood's little book of selected quotes

And she finds it difficult to believe— that a person would love her even when she isn't trying. Trying to figure out what other people need, trying to be worthy.

Margaret Atwood's little book of selected quotes

Although from you
I far must roam,
do not be broken
hearted. We two, who
in the souls are one,
are never truly
parted.

Margaret Atwood's
little book of
selected quotes

I never say I'm an
"ist" of any kind
unless I know how
the other person
is defining it.

Margaret Atwood's
little book of
selected quotes

As human beings,
we are always torn
between individual
freedom and the
ability of choose our
actions, and the need
for at least enough
social structure so
that anarchy, chaos,
and warlordery – or
the war of all against
all – can be avoided.

You can never read your own book with the innocent anticipation that comes with that first delicious page of a new book, because you wrote the thing. You've been backstage. You've seen how the rabbits were smuggled into the hat. Therefore ask a reading friend or two to look at it before you give it to anyone in the publishing business. This friend should not be someone with whom you have a romantic relationship, unless you want to break up.

Margaret Atwood's little book of selected quotes

Time is not a line but a dimension, like the dimensions of space.

Margaret Atwood's little book of selected quotes

Reality simply
consists of different
points of view.

Margaret Atwood's
little book of
selected quotes

I read for
pleasure and that
is the moment I
learn the most.

Margaret Atwood's
little book of
selected quotes

I never have [suffered writer's block], although I've had books that didn't work out. I had to stop writing them. I just abandoned them. It was depressing, but it wasn't the end of the world. When it really isn't working, and you've been bashing yourself against the wall, it's kind of a relief. I mean, sometimes you bash yourself against the wall and you get through it. But sometimes the wall is just a wall. There's nothing to be done but go somewhere else.

Margaret Atwood's little book of selected quotes

We still think of
a powerful man as
a born leader and
a powerful woman
as an anomaly.

Margaret Atwood's
little book of
selected quotes

There's always
something to occupy
the inquiring mind.

Margaret Atwood's
little book of
selected quotes

More of your brain
is involved when
reading than it is
when you watch
television...
because you are
supplying just
about everything...
you're a creator.

Margaret Atwood's
little book of
selected quotes

By now you know: I come from another planet. But I will never say to you, "Take me to your leaders." Even I--unused to your ways though I am-- would never make that mistake. We ourselves have such beings among us, made of cogs, pieces of paper, small disks of shiny metal, scraps of coloured cloth. I do not need to encounter more of them. Instead I will say, "Take me to your trees. Take me to your breakfasts, your sunsets, your bad dreams, your shoes, your nouns. Take me to your fingers; take me to your deaths." These are worth it. These are what I have come for.

Margaret Atwood's little book of selected quotes

Home is where the heart is, I thought now, gathering myself together in Betty's Luncheonette. I had no heart any more, it had been broken; or not broken, it simply wasn't there any more. It had been scooped neatly out of me like the yolk from a hard-boiled egg, leaving the rest of me bloodless and congealed and hollow. I'm heartless, I thought. Therefore I'm homeless.

Margaret Atwood's little book of selected quotes

Things musicals
taught me: All your
problems will go away
if you sing about it.

Margaret Atwood's
little book of
selected quotes

The world is being run by people my age, men my age, with falling-out hair and health worries, and it frightens me. When the leaders were older than me I could believe in their wisdom, I could believe they had transcended rage and malice and the need to be loved. Now I know better. I look at the faces in newspapers, in magazines, and wonder: what greeds, what furies drive them on?

Margaret Atwood's little book of selected quotes

I am nervous about
dogmas of any kind,
whether they be
religious,
political, or anti-
religious. Too many
heads have rolled
because of them.

Margaret Atwood's
little book of
selected quotes

And consider: it is loss to which everything flows, absence in which everything flowers

Margaret Atwood's little book of selected quotes

I don't find the idea of sewing degrading. A thing is degrading when you are forced to do it, through economic reasons or through slavery or some other form of compulsion.

Margaret Atwood's little book of selected quotes

Happiness is a garden walled with glass: there's no way in or out. In Paradise there are no stories, because there are no journeys. It's loss and regret and misery and yearning that drive the story forward, along its twisted road.

Margaret Atwood's little book of selected quotes

Screw poetry, it's you I want, your taste, rain on you, mouth on your skin.

Margaret Atwood's little book of selected quotes

Myths can't be translated as they did in their ancient soil. We can only find our own meaning in our own time.

Margaret Atwood's little book of selected quotes

A divorce is like
an amputation:
you survive it, but
there's less of you.

Margaret Atwood's
little book of
selected quotes

Water does not resist. Water flows. When you plunge your hand into it, all you feel is a caress. Water is not a solid wall, it will not stop you. But water always goes where it wants to go, and nothing in the end can stand against it. Water is patient. Dripping water wears away a stone. Remember that, my child. Remember you are half water. If you can't go through an obstacle, go around it. Water does.

Margaret Atwood's little book of selected quotes

It's a feature of our age that if you write a work of fiction, everyone assumes that the people and events in it are disguised biography — but if you write your biography, it's equally assumed you're lying your head off.

Margaret Atwood's little book of selected quotes

Our biggest
technology that we
ever, ever invented
was articulated
language with built-
out grammar. It is
that that allows us to
imagine things far in
the future and things
way back in the past.

Margaret Atwood's
little book of
selected quotes

If you're not annoying somebody, you're not really alive.

Margaret Atwood's little book of selected quotes

There are some women who seem to be born without fear, just as there are people who are born without the ability to feel pain ... Providence appears to protect such women, maybe out of astonishment.

Margaret Atwood's little book of selected quotes

I exist in two places, here and where you are.

Margaret Atwood's little book of selected quotes

Men and women are not "equal" if "equal" means "exactly the same." Our many puzzlements and indeed unhappinesses come from trying to figure out what the differences really mean, or should mean, or should not mean.

Margaret Atwood's little book of selected quotes

If we were all on trial for our thoughts, we would all be hanged.

Margaret Atwood's little book of selected quotes

Everyone thinks writers must know more about the inside of the human head, but that's wrong. They know less, that's why they write. Trying to find out what everyone else takes for granted.

Margaret Atwood's little book of selected quotes

We are a society
dying, said Aunt
Lydia, of too much
choice.

Margaret Atwood's
little book of
selected quotes

I walk away from him. It's enormously pleasing to me, this walking away. It's like being able to make people appear and vanish, at will.

Margaret Atwood's little book of selected quotes

Like the trains, she's never on time and always departing.

Margaret Atwood's little book of selected quotes

The desire to be loved
is the last illusion.
Give it up and you
will be free.

Margaret Atwood's
little book of
selected quotes

So much for endings. Beginnings are always more fun. True connoisseurs, however, are known to favor the stretch in between, since it's the hardest to do anything with. That's about all that can be said for plots, which anyway are just one thing after another, a what and a what and a what.

Margaret Atwood's little book of selected quotes

Hope drives us to invent
new fixes for old messes,
which in turn create ever
more dangerous messes.
Hope elects the politician
with the biggest empty
promise; and as any
stockbroker or lottery
seller knows, most of us
will take a slim hope over
prudent and predictable
frugality. Hope, like
greed, fuels the engine
of capitalism.

Margaret Atwood's
little book of
selected quotes

Another belief of
mine; that everyone
else my age is an
adult, whereas I am
merely in disguise.

Margaret Atwood's
little book of
selected quotes

Anybody who writes a book is an optimist. First of all, they think they're going to finish it. Second, they think somebody's going to publish it. Third, they think somebody's going to read it. Fourth, they think somebody's going to like it. How optimistic is that?

Margaret Atwood's little book of selected quotes

You cannot teach somebody to write a masterpiece, but you can certainly teach them how to improve their writing skills. And you can teach them that they can make their own voices more effective by being able to communicate more clearly and forcefully. It makes people feel more capable when they can write – for instance to make a request – of a politician – and when they are able to receive a reply.

Margaret Atwood's little book of selected quotes

Hatred would have been easier. With hatred, I would have known what to do. Hatred is clear, metallic, one-handed, unwavering; unlike love.

Margaret Atwood's little book of selected quotes

You can only be
jealous of someone
who has something
you think you ought
to have yourself.

Margaret Atwood's
little book of
selected quotes

My own view of myself
was that I was small
and innocuous, a
marshmallow compared
to the others. I was a
poor shot with a 22,
for instance, and not
very good with an ax.
It took me a long time
to figure out that the
youngest in a family
of dragons is still a
dragon from the point
of view of those who
find dragons alarming.

We're facing growing climate change, more floods, more droughts, more crisis on a planetary level, and the systems we put in place in the twentieth century are just not going to work. We've run out of stuff. Our big problems are going to be energy supplies and food supplies. This is not a right-left issue.

There's the story, then there's the real story, then there's the story of how the story came to be told. Then there's what you leave out of the story. Which is part of the story too.

Margaret Atwood's little book of selected quotes

Inside the peach,
there is a stone.

Margaret Atwood's
little book of
selected quotes

All it takes," said Crake, "is the elimination of one generation. One generation of anything. Beetles, trees, microbes, scientists, speakers of French, whatever. Break the link in time between one generation and the next, and it's game over forever.

Margaret Atwood's little book of selected quotes

The fabric of
democracy is always
fragile everywhere
because it depends on
the will of citizens
to protect it, and
when they become
scared, when it
becomes dangerous for
them to defend it, it
can go very quickly.

Margaret Atwood's
little book of
selected quotes

Oppression involves a failure of the imagination: the failure to imagine the full humanity of other human beings.

Margaret Atwood's little book of selected quotes

Stupidity is the same
as evil if you judge
by the results.

Margaret Atwood's
little book of
selected quotes

What I need is perspective.
The illusion of depth, created
by a frame, the arrangement of
shapes on a flat surface.
Perspective is necessary.
Otherwise there are only two
dimensions. Otherwise you
live with your face squashed
up against a wall, everything
a huge foreground, of details,
close-ups, hairs, the weave of
the bedsheet, the molecules of
the face. Your own skin like a
map, a diagram of futility,
criscrossed with tiny roads
that lead nowhere. Otherwise
you live in the moment. Which
is not where I want to be.

Margaret Atwood's
little book of
selected quotes

Winning
intoxicates you,
and numbs you to
the sufferings of
others.

Margaret Atwood's
little book of
selected quotes

I hope that people will finally come to realize that there is only one 'race' – the human race – and that we are all members of it.

Margaret Atwood's little book of selected quotes

Show me a character totally without anxieties and I will show you a boring book.

Margaret Atwood's little book of selected quotes

The sands of time are quicksands ... so much can sink into them without a trace.

Margaret Atwood's little book of selected quotes

We yearned for the future. How did we learn it, that talent for insatiability?

I'm not sure which
is worse: intense
feeling, or the
absence of it.

Margaret Atwood's
little book of
selected quotes

he might die for her,
but living for her
would be quite
different.

Margaret Atwood's
little book of
selected quotes

Publishing a book is like stuffing a note into a bottle and hurling it into the sea. Some bottles drown, some come safe to land, where the notes are read and then possibly cherished, or else misinterpreted, or else understood all too well by those who hate the message. You never know who your readers might be.

Good writing takes place at intersections, at what you might call knots, at places where the society is snarled or knotted up.

Margaret Atwood's little book of selected quotes

Made in the USA
Las Vegas, NV
07 September 2022